BUILD POSITIVE HABITS NOW

HACKNEY AND JONES

© **Copyright 2021 - All rights reserved.**

The content contained within this book may not be reproduced, duplicated or transmitted without direct written permission from the author or the publisher.

Under no circumstances will any blame or legal responsibility be held against the publisher, or author, for any damages, reparation, or monetary loss due to the information contained within this book, either directly or indirectly.

Legal Notice:

Note that this book is copyright protected. It is only for personal use. You cannot amend, distribute, sell, use, quote or paraphrase any part, or the content within this book, without the consent of the author or publisher.

By reading this document, the reader agrees that under no circumstances is the author responsible for any losses, direct or indirect, that are incurred as a result of the use of information contained within this document, including, but not limited to, errors, omissions, or inaccuracies.

Claim Your Freebie NOW!

Get Good At Problem Solving

Want to know the secret behind getting good at problem solving? Everyone seems to be able to do it, but you're stuck in the pile of endless to-do lists with little progress.

Ok, so how do I get my FREE book?

EASY! See the next page

Claim Your Freebie NOW

Instructions:

1. Open the camera or the QR reader application on your smartphone.
2. Point your camera at the QR code to scan the QR code.
3. A notification will pop-up on screen.
4. Click on the notification to open the website link

Contents

1. Why are you here? — 1
2. What is a habit? — 2
3. What is a positive habit? — 4
4. Benefits of a positive habit — 7
5. Examples of positive habits of famous people — 9
6. Why don't we stick to positive habits? — 13
7. Tips to start sticking to positive habits — 15
8. What are the best habits to have and why? — 17
9. Examples of daily habits — 21
10. Examples of monthly habits — 23
11. Mental Health habits — 25
12. Exercise habits — 28
13. Workplace habits — 31

Feedback — 33

1

Why are you here?

WHILE MOST PEOPLE look forward to building a positive habit, seeing it as a way to live a successful and rewarding life, that quest also comes with many challenges and drawbacks—these range from lack of determination, discipline, commitment, consistency, and patience. While the latter is one of the most neglected prerequisites, there is, however, very little information about the nitty-gritty of building positive habits.

Hence, in this book, you will be exposed to everything you need to know about building positive habits. Also, by the end of this book, you will be aware of various positive habits and their benefits.

So I urge you to take your time and read it carefully and trust me you will enjoy and understand it!

2

What is a habit?

HABITS ARE OFTEN LEARNED hence can be built (although sometimes one might need to be unrelenting, and lots of habits are on autopilot). To successfully make habits, we've got to understand what we're dealing with. What then is a habit? The Merriam-Webster dictionary defines a habit as "a behaviour pattern acquired by frequent repetition or physiologic exposure that shows itself in regularity or increased performance facility." The Macmillan dictionary also defines a habit as "something that you do often or regularly, often without thinking about it". Thus we can resolve that habits are routine behaviours done daily.

They are recurrent and often unconscious patterns of behaviour and are acquired through prevailing repetition. Numerous of these are unconscious, so we don't even realise we are engaging in them. Thus we can see that habits outline our character, thoughts, feelings, and 'usual' behaviours.

Additionally, we can see that habits are behaviours that are nearly or entirely involuntary, and since they're often recurring, we tend to become improved at them (increased facility of performance). From a psychological perspective, a habit may also be thought of as a connection between a stimulus and a reaction.

It serves as a mental affiliation between a trigger thought or event (stimulus) and response to its trigger (the answer). Continuance with this mental affiliation time and again forms a habit and affects all accompanying choices and actions.

A habit may also be associated with addiction. Some people believe the term addiction should be reserved for describing a physical dependency on chemical substances like alcohol and medicines. Other addictions include various compulsive behaviours like gambling, eating, shopping, taking part in video games, work, and usage of the internet. However, how do habits work? Firstly, there's a trigger or cue (e.g., location, time of day, spirit, thought, belief, others, or a pattern of behaviour) that then triggers a routine. You get the reward you desire (identity what reward is driving your habit, perhaps what are you desiring or avoiding).

Since a habit could be a frequently recurring action, you can deliberately build whatsoever habits by selecting an activity and implementing a technique to perform it often. Examples of habits are reading, meditating, using the gym, studying, gambling, smoking, praying, doing exercise, drinking alcohol, sleeping, stalking, writing, procrastination, daydreaming, punctuality etc.

3

What is a positive habit?

HIGHLY SUCCESSFUL PEOPLE often attribute their success to specific habits that they maintain. Performing particular actions regularly can have a beneficial impact on one's career and progress toward goals. Hence, a positive pattern is an adopted or acquired positive behaviour or action.

It's not difficult to develop positive habits. The problem lies in that we have no plan or structure or any idea about how to set about it. Here are some examples of positive habits that you may wish to have:

1. Read books.

Reading is an awesome habit to create that can positively influence one's creative thinking, analytical skills, cognition, and stress levels. The act of reading for quite some minutes every day can lower one's heart rate, relieve stress, and aid one to sleep healthier.

2. Connect with others.

Building and maintaining positive relationships can have a significant impact on one's career. Positive relationships outside of one's workplace contribute to a healthy work-life balance. Forming great business relationships with colleagues and business contacts can assist one to have a pleasant work setting.

3. Set and pursue goals.

Identifying, designing, and trailing progress toward one's career goals can be a habit that can result in success. These actions encompass other habits of the successful individual such as living purposefully, taking action, avoiding dawdling, and being goal-oriented or results-driven.

4. Develop a healthy lifestyle.

Living a healthy lifestyle involves eating healthy food, obtaining enough rest at night, and working out often. These habits can provide energy and stamina to come back refreshed and prepared to accomplish one's tasks.

5. Challenge yourself.

Regularly encouraging oneself to move outside of one's comfort zone and seek out or go for new challenges can lead one to learn new skills, accept additional responsibility, earn a promotion, and assist one to keep working toward one's goals.

6. Be updated and informed.

Very successful individuals are usually up-to-date in their field or career. Staying conscious of news, technology, current trends, or research can assist one to perform well in one's role, pick out market opportunities, and know-how best to manage any circumstance.

. . .

7. Organise your finances.

One key to success is being in control of one's finances at all times. Highly successful individuals often live within their financial capability, invest well or create multiple financial gain streams. Organisation can be helpful in each sphere of career success. Organising one's finances well can assist one in identifying and targeting one's desired job.

8. Utilise feedback.

Habitually getting feedback can bring about career success by assisting one to discover one's strengths and weaknesses. Implement the feedback by making plans to use your strengths often or improve your weaknesses.

9. Maintain a routine.

The most common habit of highly successful individuals is to possess a daily routine. Building and maintaining a routine for every part of one's day can assist one to work toward one's goals, engage in positive actions, and ascertain one's productivity.

You can build any positive habit if you're consistent enough to adopt a few actions repeatedly for some time. You produce steady positive habits by repeating a particular helpful action throughout a given period, with a guideline to support you in achieving what you want.

4

Benefits of a positive habit

THE FASCINATING THING regarding positive habits is that they can be built. It may be challenging to give up old habits. It seems the worst habits are the toughest to stop; however, it's accomplishable. If you want to start taking a healthy diet, all you have got to do is skip your morning doughnut till it becomes habitual to refuse pastries at breakfast.

Positive habits enable you to achieve your goals. The first step of reaching any goal is establishing a daily routine. If you would like an improved job, you need to begin the daily routine of searching for work. If you would like to lift three hundred pounds, you need to start the daily routine of lifting weights. Positive habits set a foundation throughout life since habits become you; the positive habits that you opt to build set the tone for your entire life.

Habits are the first step of your life setup. If you have got a life goal, it isn't the plan itself that may assist you in reaching your dreams; it's the habits that you just build and follow while you're attempting to get there.

As humans, we tend to waste loads of our time. Most individuals would instead not do something demanding or challenging. However, if we build positive habits, we tend to become more competent, reducing the time we have wasted. Positive habits can substitute motivation.

We all have days when we just don't feel like exercising, working, or eating well.

However, when these things are positive habits, they become part and parcel of us, and we do them without hesitating.

Additionally, relying on the findings of leading researchers and experts on habit and self-discipline, we can point to other benefits of positive habits such as improved health, longer life, enhanced self-esteem, coping more effectively with stress, increased happiness, better professional success, improved focus and better confidence.

5

Examples of positive habits of famous people

MOST SUCCESSFUL INDIVIDUALS have several things in common. For example, most of them agree that the first action in the morning is to 'eat a frog'. This implies that it is better to handle the most discouraging and disgusting activities on the list immediately after waking up.

Among other characteristics of their daily routine, there's typically a well-balanced and strictly organised daily schedule that helps them thrive in their careers and private lives. I have compiled ten habits of famous people you should adopt to turn your life into a success.

1. Oprah Winfrey: Meditation.

The benefits of meditating are well-known to several individuals. It helps reduce back stress, boost creativity, improve productivity and maintain general well-being. That's why Oprah Winfrey usually includes meditation in her daily routine. Oprah starts every morning with twenty minutes of sitting meditation, not skipping holidays and weekends. She says that sitting in stillness fills her with hope, a sense of happiness, and deep joy.

. . .

2. Jennifer Aniston: Rise early.

You've most likely noticed that almost all successful individuals are early birds, and Jennifer Aniston is no exception here. Each workday, she gets up at 4:30 AM and instantly starts doing her morning rituals. Rising early enables her to induce a vantage on the day and have some quality time for herself before going to work.

3. Lea Michele: Take a steam shower.

Each morning after a cup of coffee, Lea Michele takes a steam shower. She steams for a long while on even her busiest days because this procedure helps her rebuff and sweat out all of the toxins from her body.

4. Richard Branson: Spend time together with your family.

It seems that Branson isn't the only early bird in his family. Regardless of his schedule, Richard wakes up at around five AM, exercises, and grabs his breakfast. However, the essential part of his morning is communing with his family. Branson says that some quality family time puts him in an exceedingly excellent frame of mind before executing his daily business.

5. Jessica Alba: Exercise or work out with your friends.

All successful individuals recognise the importance of physical activities and working out. Jessica Alba found a therapy out of this circumstance. She uses her workout friends to assist her in turning early morning sweat sessions into a reality. The actress admits that working out isn't her favourite activity. However, it helps her cut back stress, and her friends constantly make her enthusiastic to try and do some yoga or spinning classes.

. . .

6. Bretagne Snow: Creating your "getting ready playlist".

Even if you always rise on the wrong side of the bed, you can conveniently modify your negative mood into a positive one by employing some nice tunes. The Pitch Perfect star Bretagne Snow calls it a "getting-ready" list. As a rule, after breakfast, she puts on her playlist filled with fascinating and mood-boosting songs that she blasts on the speakers throughout her house.

7. Julianne Hough: Be thankful.

Julianne Hough prefers to start her day positively by exhibiting her morning gratitude ritual. Early at 6:30 AM, she sits up in her bed and thinks of five things she's grateful for that either already happened to her or that she desires to do that day. Only after this does she get out of bed, brush her teeth, and continues with her morning routines.

8. Kate Hudson: Make an ice bath for your face.

Kate Hudson typically wakes up with the aid of an ice bath. She acquired this habit from a makeup artist she worked with and began to do it each morning. This freezing bath wakes her up very quickly and softens her facial skin, and provides her with a glow.

9. Steve Jobs: Always remind yourself of your dreams.

In his speech to some graduating students at Stanford, Jobs stated that every morning he looked in the mirror and asked himself the same question: "If this day was the last day of my life, would I still try and do what I'm doing today?" Whenever his answer was "no" for several days in a row, he was sure that he was required to change something in his life. This type of reappraisal of his work and needs every single day assisted him in pursuing his dreams while not forgetting about his true self.

10. Mark Zuckerberg: Obviate choices.

Of course, having countless choices could seem awful and even luxurious for a few people. However, once you're in haste in the morning, wasting those precious minutes on deciding what to wear or to eat may very well make your day a whole disaster. That's why successful and affluent individuals have voluntarily chosen to eliminate their choices throughout the day. An example of this is seen by Mark Zuckerberg, who admits that he has about twenty similar grey T-shirts in his closet. This lack of selection helps him avoid decision fatigue and focus his attention on business.

6

Why don't we stick to positive habits?

Do you find yourself beginning a new routine several times but never quite getting it to stick? You attempt to set up systems and daily habits, but every time, they don't work. You start to feel like a failed person.

The problem isn't centred on task setup and time management. It's all in your head, and here's why. When you try to stick to a positive habit but don't believe you'll achieve it, you have failed even before you even begin. There's a small but powerful voice inside you murmuring that you're not fit for this, and who are you even to try. Why is it difficult to stick to positive habits? Why is it so hard to make an invariable change?

How can we have the best intentions to become better and nonetheless still see so slight improvement? And most importantly, is there anything we can do about it? Your life goals are not your habits. Sticking to positive habits requires determination, patience, and consistency.

If you don't make the time, it won't happen.

Whatever that first step is toward making progress on your positive habits, commit and work towards it. Commit and practice. Giving up is easy. Seeing it through is worth it.

We all have hopes and ambitions, and often time, we have

at least a general insight of what those goals are: the way we want our bodies to look and the good health we want to enjoy, the respect we want to get from our peers, and the vital work we want to produce, the relationships we want with our family, friends, colleagues and the love we want to share.

Overall, this is a good thing.

It's good to know what you want, and having dreams gives you a sense of direction and purpose. Nonetheless, if you are not a committed, disciplined, and committed individual, you cannot stick to positive habits

7

Tips to start sticking to positive habits

TOO OFTEN, we tend to let our motivations and wishes drive us into delirium as we tend to solve our entire problems promptly rather than beginning a small, new routine.

Hence, how do we balance our need to create life-changing transformations with the necessity to stick to positive, sustainable habits? Here are two tips that can help you stick to positive habits:

1. Dream big, however, start small.

If you're serious about making real change, then you have to start small. Imagine the regular habits, positive or negative: Putting your seatbelt on, biting your nails, brushing your teeth. These actions are small enough that you don't even think about them. You simply do them in a reflex manner.

They are tiny actions that become conformable patterns. Wouldn't it make sense that if we wanted to stick to a new positive habit, the best way to start would be to make tiny changes that our brain could promptly learn and automatically repeat?

What if you started thinking of your life goals, not as big, dauntless things that you can only achieve at the right time or when you have better resources but instead as tiny, daily behaviours that are repeated until success becomes ineluctable?

I think the following quote from B.J. Fogg, a professor at Stanford University, explains this idea clearly, "If you plant the right seed in the right spot, it will grow without further coaxing." I consider this as the best metaphor for sticking to positive habits.

2. Concentrate on life-*style*, not life-changing.

Too often, we tend to get obsessed with making life-changing transformations.

Losing 30 pounds would be life-changing; drinking six glasses of water every day is a new type of lifestyle. Publishing your first book would be life-changing; emailing a new book agent daily is a new type of lifestyle. Do you notice the difference?

Life goals are reasonable because they provide guidance, but they can also trick you into assuming more than you can handle. Daily habits, tiny routines that are repeatable, are what make big ambitions a reality.

8

What are the best habits to have and why?

WE OFTEN FEEL that we can do better, and we want to do better. But somehow, situations and our lives make us think as if we cannot change, at least not without great efforts.

This is untrue. Some of our old and new habits, which run at least 40% of our daily life on an automated mode, need a more significant chunk of time than we have. But regardless of how dense some of these practices sound, they all need a starting point that could be a few minutes.

Hoping for "the big break" is not only unavailing, but it is also risky because it keeps you from taking the actions you need to produce the results you want". We don't have to wait for an ideal one hour. Waiting for that one hour is holding us up from attaining our goal. We get it; it's hard to stop bad habits.

But when it comes to building positive habits, small decisions add up over time. Below is my compilation of the best habits to have and why you should have them:

1. Say something nice to your loved one when you wake up. Acknowledge their presence in your life. This brings about an affectionate atmosphere.

. . .

2. Replace diet soft drinks with carbonated water. Research suggests the brain reacts to artificial sweeteners much as it does to sugary sweets. Going cold turkey seems unrealistic, but if you start decreasing the amount of diet soft drinks and artificial sweeteners you take, your waistline and health will improve.

3. Try taking a 10-minute walk. If you're at work, walk to the furthest bathroom and take the stairs. While running errands, try to find the most distant parking space and walk from there. Remember, even the smallest amount of steps still add up.

4. Integrate balance exercises into your routine. Balance on one leg for ten seconds at a time, then switch to the other leg. It's a part of neuro-motor training, which helps you improve your balance, agility, and mobility, all things you need in everyday movement and other forms of exercise.

5. Weigh yourself weekly. To keep your weight from creeping up on you, set a weekly maintenance or loss goal for yourself, write it down, and check yourself against that goal. Weigh yourself every week on the same day and at the same time, and make sure you wear the same amount of clothing for consistency.

6. Begin your day with a healthy breakfast. Eat food high in fibre that includes protein to keep you full and energised. If you begin the day correctly, there is a tendency for you to eat better overall, and it helps lower your risk of diabetes and improves heart health. Not only that, eating breakfast helps

reduce brain fog, so you'll be ready to go for those morning meetings.

7. Find creative substitutions for unhealthy foods. Try to do away with meals and snacks that you regularly buy that are high in calories but low on their health benefit. Eat them less often as an occasional treat. Try using low-fat dairy, healthy oils like avocado, whole grains, olive oil, and natural sweeteners like fruit instead of high fat or sugary meals.

8. Irrespective of the time you wake up, work out for at least ten minutes. Do five if you can't do ten. Apart from keeping us fit, exercise reduces stress and elates our mood. The uplifting effects of exercising overflows in every part of our day, making everything seem a bit better.

9. Sit silently for about ten minutes. Don't have ten minutes? Keep everything aside, and calm yourself for five minutes—one of the easiest habits. Even though a wandering mind is an unhappy mind, research shows that forty-seven per cent of the time, people are thinking about something else other than what they are working on. But what has meditation got to do with focus? It is established that long-term meditators can bring their focus back much more quickly than non-meditators.

10. Appreciate yourself for the things you have done and achieved so far. You are already a master of your day. Think good thoughts about yourself. Profess positive things about yourself. Look at yourself in the mirror and smile. Small wins like starting a day on the right note and taking care of your-

self would convince you that better results are close by. Be thankful to yourself. It makes you optimistic.

11. Finish your day by writing down the priorities for the following day. Humans love control. Having a sense of tomorrow calms us. If you don't have a to-do list, you might fluff in the morning while delaying your most crucial task. If you have a task list, you can get straight to your work. Having a task list is a positive habit that will help you plan your other tasks and even achieve your daily goals before time.

12. Read a book. Aside from the vast knowledge you gain while reading, reading unwinds us immensely. And imagine how much you would have read in a year if you go through five pages a day of a good book? Well, 1825 pages!

9

Examples of daily habits

HERE ARE examples of positive daily habits that can help you become highly productive:

1. Give yourself more time by waking up earlier.

2. Set your most important tasks for the day.

3. Make your bed.

4. Connect with your bigger goals by recording them.

5. Meditate in preparation for whatever the day brings.

6. Eat the frog (tackle something difficult when your energy is the fullest).

7. Schedule (and take) more breaks.

8. Set hard limits on definite activities.

9. Reflect on your accomplishments and get motivation from them.

10. Create time for mental solitude.

11. Spend time on a hobby.

12. Prepare for tomorrow with a 'shutdown ritual'.

13. Turn off your devices at least thirty minutes before bed, and don't keep them close to you.

14. Give your eyes a break. Meditation is one way to do that.

15. Drink more water during the day. Make this a regular habit.

16. Exercise regularly. Exercise makes us fit and healthy.

10

Examples of monthly habits

HERE ARE examples of positive monthly habits that can make your month productive:

1. Sticking to your goals and plan and executing them without spilling them over into the next month.

2. Avoiding extravagant spending when you get paid.

3. Doing something different towards achieving a long-term goal.

4. Relearning and unlearning previous lessons.

5. Reminiscing on mistakes in the past months and making conscious moves not to repeat them.

. . .

6. Analysing your financial budget.

7. Preparing a diet plan.

8. Taking time out for leisure activities.

11

Mental Health habits

OUR LIVES ARE OFTEN OCCUPIED and full of stress all the time. If you've ever gone through periods of high anxiety, you know how much it can affect not only your physical health but also your mental health. Discovering ways to keep yourself still and relaxed can help keep stress from taking control of your life. Although you may feel lost in the fight against the unforeseen difficulty of everyday stress, there are mental habits that can help you cope and keep yourself as healthy as possible. Here are five to start:

1. Get enough sleep.

Sleep is essential because it permits your body to rest and refreshes your mind. Sleep can also affect your mood. If you aren't allowing yourself to get plenty of rest at night, you can quickly become fractious, and your physical health may deteriorate along with your mental wellbeing.

2. Eat healthy food and exercise regularly.

Eating correctly is significant for many reasons, but did

you know it can affect you mentally? By eating good and healthy foods full of life-sustaining nutrients, you increase your overall wellbeing and reduce anxiety and stress. Exercise goes together with healthy eating, as it can also improve your overall mood and fight anxiety and depression by relinquishing the feel-good hormones serotonin and dopamine.

3. Be social and find connection with others.

Social interaction is a very distinct part of being human. It allows you to connect with people of all kinds on different levels. Building connections with others, whether family, friends, or colleagues, can help you fight the stressors that creep up on you every day. You can even stretch outside of your actual circle and get involved in the community or volunteer to help boost your mood and the way you relate to people.

4. Create time to relax.

By and by, stress can accumulate in your body and wreak havoc on your mind. One of the best ways to fight this is by training your mind actively to relax. This decreases stress levels, reduces muscle tension, and reduces blood pressure. A good relaxation technique is meditation. Meditation takes practice, but it's a very effective tool in fighting difficult or trying times in your life.

5. Learn to be grateful and stay positive.

Recalling that you have things to be thankful for in your life is just as significant as eating healthy and exercising. Gratitude is a fantastic way to have a positive mindset when life is challenging you and you become mentally down.

Set some time aside each day to think about the positives

in your life and write them down so you can refer to them. And having a positive mindset on life, even in your darkest moments, can help your mental health to an exceedingly great extent.

12

Exercise habits

DAILY EXERCISE IS a positive habit that is essential for a healthy mind and body. Developing healthy habits is easier said than done. Most people want to be healthy. We know the things we should do to be healthy, such as exercise. A lot of people are motivated to adopt an exercise plan. Sometimes they are not just committed to doing the work it takes to sustain a change. Experts have several different methods for building habits. Some of them say getting involved in an activity for 21 days without interruption will make it a habit. Others recommend setting clearly defined goals. Here are a few exercise habits:

1. Get credible information on exercise.

Before beginning an exercise routine, talk to an exercise physiologist or an expert. This is important if you have not been active, have health problems, pregnant or if you are an older adult. Ask your doctor about how much exercise is right for you.

A good target for many people is to work up to exercising three times a week for thirty to sixty minutes at a time.

And if thirty to sixty minutes at a time sounds challenging

to fit into a busy schedule, you can split up your physical activity into smaller periods. Exercise has so many health benefits that any amount is better than none.

2. Take the stairs instead of the lift at work.

3. Go for a walk during your lunch break.

4. Do housework at a snappy pace.

5. Dance while you are listening to music.

6. Put *exercise appointments* on your calendar. This helps you remember your appointments.

7. Keep a daily log or diary of your exercise activities.

8. Schedule regular active household chores that require you to be more active. Make it a series of organised activities.

9. Check your progress. Can you walk a certain distance faster now? Are you at your target heart rate? Take note of the feedback.

10. Think about joining a health club or community centre. The cost might allow you to exercise regularly. Registering for

a class or meeting with a trainer can also keep you accountable.

11. Think of the benefits of regular exercise. Write down the services and goals, and keep them pinned somewhere you can easily see them. This serves as a form of motivation to keep up with the habit.

13

Workplace habits

YOU MUST ALWAYS REMEMBER that positive work habits enhance success.

It's necessary to develop and maintain excellent work habits. If consistently maintained, good work habits drive success, resulting in an employee contributing more, adding to their job satisfaction while creating better relationships between peers, colleagues, and superiors.

HERE ARE positive work habits that will contribute to the best possible experience at work:

1. Learn to adopt and even seek out constructive feedback.

2. Create solutions, not problems and difficulties.

3. Be organised and coordinated.

. . .

4. Be dependable.

5. Assign more time than you think you need to everything.

6. Be inquisitive.

7. Be humble and willing to admit your ignorance.

8. Ask for and offer help.

9. Always do your best with all sincerity.

10. Go above and beyond.

11. Be kind and considerate.

12. Look at problems as opportunities.

13. Keep personal problems out of the workplace.

14. Stop procrastinating.

15. Listen to people carefully.

Feedback

Thank you for reading 'Build Positive Habits Now'. We sincerely hope you enjoyed and got value from this book, and that it helps you to forge those all-important positive habits that will bring peace and harmony to your life from this moment on.

If you have a free moment, please leave us some feedback on Amazon.

Also, scan the QR code below to visit our website where you can find more information on our range of books available.

 HackneyandJones.com